CW00862454

1-The first bicycle ...
by Karl Drais in 1817, and it was called a "horseless racing machine".

2-The "peloton" can cover more than 100 kilometers in one hour during the flat stages of the Tour de France.

3-The Tour de France is the most famous cycling race in the world and was created in 1903.

4-The bike used by British rider Chris Boardman to set the hour record in 1996 had carbon wheels, an aerodynamic shape, and a streamlined headset.

5-Eddy Merckx is widely considered the greatest cyclist of all time, having won 11 Grand Tours and 19 monumental classics.

6-German rider Jan Ullrich was the only one to beat Lance Armstrong during his winning streak at the Tour de France.

7-The first track bicycle race took place in Paris in 1868.

8-The "Madison" is a team track cycling event where riders take turns to score points.

9-The most expensive bicycle in the world was created by British artist Damien Hirst and costs more than $500,000.

10-The bicycle was first used as a means of transport in Switzerland in the 19th century.

11-The largest peloton of cyclists recorded in a race occurred during Paris-Roubaix in 2010, with 210 riders.

12-The famous "Milan-San Remo" cycling race is the longest one-day classic on the professional calendar, with more than 290 kilometers.

13-The fastest cyclist in the world on the flat is the Dutchman Fred Rompelberg, who reached a speed of 268.831 km/h in 1995.

14-The first women's Tour de France took place in 1984, but it did not last long due to lack of funding.

15-The term "peloton" is of French origin and means "small ball" due to the compact shape of the riders grouped together.

16-The Vélodrome de Roubaix, located in France, is famous for being the finish site of the Paris-Roubaix race, known for its cobblestones.

17-The total distance covered by a rider during an edition of the Tour de France is approximately 3,500 kilometers.

18-Professional runners typically consume between 5,000 and 7,000 calories per day during Grand Tours.

19-Disc brakes are now allowed in most professional races, despite some controversy.

20-Italian rider Fausto Coppi is one of the few to have won the Tour de France and the Giro d'Italia in the same year, accomplishing this feat in 1949 and 1952.

21-The hour record is an event where a cyclist attempts to cover the greatest distance possible in one hour. The current record is held by Victor Campenaerts, with 55.089 kilometers in 2019.

22-The Paris-Roubaix race is nicknamed "The Hell of the North" because of its difficult cobbled sections.

23-Early bicycles had wooden wheels and were extremely uncomfortable compared to modern bicycles.

24-The concept of the "automatic pedal" was invented by the Frenchman Charles Hanson in 1895.

25-The first woman to complete the Tour de France was Alfonsina Strada in 1924. She had been registered under a male name, Alfonsin Strada, but was later discovered.

26-Bikes used for time trials feature low-profile wheels, aero handlebars, and full body suits to reduce drag.

27-Tubular tires are preferred by many professional racers due to their light weight and ability to be repaired more easily.

28-Italian cyclist Gino Bartali hid false identity papers to save Jews during World War II.

29-The record for the longest distance traveled in 24 hours is 941.873 kilometers, established by Oskar Persson in 1935.

30-The "Brompton World Championship" is a folding bicycle race where participants are required to wear formal clothing.

31-The oldest cyclist to complete the Tour de France was Firmin Lambot, who was 49 when he completed the race in 1922.

32-The first road cycling world championship took place in 1927 and was won by Alfredo Binda.

33-Famous rider Lance Armstrong won the Tour de France seven times in a row before his titles were stripped from him due to doping scandals.

34-The 100 kilometer race is one of the classic events of track cycling, and the first race of this type took place in 1878.

35-The longest continuous cycling event is Paris-Brest-Paris, a 1,200 kilometer ride which has taken place every four years since 1891.

36-The term "gruppetto" is used to describe a small group of riders who break away from the main peloton during a mountainous stage.

37-The Tour de France was canceled during the two world wars (1915-1918 and 1940-1946).

38-The "Vuelta a España" is another of the Grand Tours of cycling, which was created in 1935.

39-The record for climbing Mont Ventoux, a famous mountain in the Tour de France, is 55 minutes and 51 seconds, set by Iban Mayo in 2004.

40-The longest stage victory in the Tour de France is 361 kilometers, achieved by Gustave Garrigou in 1910.

41-The Tour de France is also called "La Grande Boucle" because of its circular shape.

42-The world record for the highest bicycle jump is 4.03 meters, set by Rick Koekoek in 2011.

43-The use of bicycle helmets has become compulsory in most professional races for safety reasons.

44-French rider Jacques Anquetil won the first individual time trial of the Tour de France in 1961.

45-Women were first allowed to compete at the Olympic Games in road cycling in 1984.

46-The bicycle used for track cycling is often called a "track bike" and usually does not have brakes.

47-The highest speed record achieved during a downhill mountain bike ride is 167.6 km/h, achieved by Eric Barone in 2002.

48-Italian runner Eros Poli is one of the tallest tall runners, standing at 1.96 meters tall.

49-Cyclists cover on average more than 3,000 kilometers per month during their training.

50-The hour record in disabled cycling is 45.563 kilometers, established by Andrea Eskau in 2015.

51-The world speed record for cycling without drafting (behind a vehicle) is 296 km/h, established by Todd Reichert in 2016.

52-The Tour de France introduced the white jersey for the best young rider in 1975.

53-The term "yellow jersey" of the Tour de France is so named because of the color of the newspaper L'Auto, which organized the race at the time.

54-French rider Raymond Poulidor was nicknamed "the eternal second" because of his numerous second places in the Tour de France.

55-Time trial bikes are specially designed to minimize air resistance and maximize speed.

56-The tandem time trial is a special event where two riders pedal together on a single bike.

57-Cycling is one of the most complete sports in terms of muscles used, as it involves the legs, core, arms and shoulders.

58-The distinctive polka dot jersey of the Tour de France has been awarded to the best climber since 1975.

59-The greatest number of stage victories at the Tour de France belongs to Eddy Merckx, with 34 stage victories.

60-The "Tour de Suisse" is a major cycling race which began in 1933.

61-The first bicycles did not have pedals, riders had to push the ground with their feet to move forward.

62-The hour record for a recumbent bike is 91.556 kilometers, established by Sam Whittingham in 2009.

63-The heaviest bicycle in the world weighs more than 1,000 kilograms.

64-The "Giro Rosa" is the most important women's cycling stage race and was created in 1988.

65-The first Tours de France were organized to increase the sale of the newspaper L'Auto, hence the name of the race.

66-Australian rider Cadel Evans was the first Australian to win the Tour de France in 2011.

67-The youngest cyclist to take part in the Tour de France was Maurice Garin, aged 19 during the first edition in 1903.

68-The Manchester Velodrome is famous for its track cycling competitions and hosted the Track Cycling World Championships in 2000.

69-The bicycle handlebar was invented by John Kemp Starley in 1888.

70-Norway is the country of origin of rider Thor Hushovd, world road cycling champion in 2010.

71-The track cycling event called "Keirin" was developed in Japan.

72-American cyclist Kristin Armstrong (no relation to Lance Armstrong) won three Olympic gold medals in time trials.

73-The folding bicycle was invented by Mikael Pedersen in 1893.

74-Leather bicycle saddles were common in the early 20th century before the introduction of plastic and foam saddles.

75-The bicycle was the first means of transport to reach the speed of 20 km/h.

76-The longest stage cycling race in the world is the "Tour of Africa," which covers more than 12,000 kilometers in four months.

77-The first bicycle derailleurs were invented at the beginning of the 20th century.

78-The Tour de France saw several unexpected winners, including Federico Bahamontes, the "Eagle of Toledo," who was an excellent climber.

79-The record for climbing Alpe d'Huez, a legendary mountain in the Tour de France, is 37 minutes and 35 seconds, set by Marco Pantani in 1997.

80-The bicycle is one of the most ecological means of transport, producing no greenhouse gases.

81-Professional cycling teams travel approximately 30,000 kilometers per year in competition.

82-The "Tour de Flandre" is a cycling classic that includes many steep climbs and cobbled sections in Belgium.

83-The "Penny Farthing" bicycle is one of the first bicycle models and is characterized by its large front wheel.

84-The rainbow jersey is worn by the road cycling world champion.

85-Belgian rider Axel Merckx is the son of Eddy Merckx and also had a successful cycling career.

86-Italian cyclist Gino Bartali won the Tour de France in 1938 and 1948.

87-The Tour de France visited 36 countries other than France during its departures or stages.

88-Track cycling includes events such as speed, pursuit and keirin.

89-The record for the longest distance traveled in a year is 86,573 kilometers, set by Kurt Searvogel in 2015.

90-The first bicycle helmets were made of leather and did not become compulsory until the mid-20th century.

91-The distinctive jerseys of the Tour de France are the yellow jersey (leader), the green jersey (best sprinter), the polka dot jersey (best climber), and the white jersey (best young person).

92-Group cycling is often called "drafting" and allows cyclists to reduce air resistance by following each other closely.

93-The designer of the yellow jersey for the Tour de France, Henri Desgrange, chose this color to represent the newspaper L'Auto, but also to symbolize the yellow of the stationery used by the newspaper.

94-The world record for the longest wheelie on a bicycle is more than 300 kilometers, established by Kurt Osburn in 1998.

95-The Grand Prix des Nations was a renowned individual time trial event and was nicknamed "The Chrono of Chronos".

96-Belgian brothers Edouard and André Michelin, founders of the Michelin tire company, contributed to the development of removable bicycle tires.

97-American rider Greg LeMond was the first non-European to win the Tour de France in 1986.

98-The "Tour de Romandie" is a stage race in Switzerland which began in 1947.

99-Bicycle tires are inflated to much higher pressures than car tires, typically between 80 and 130 psi (pounds per square inch).

100-The world record for the highest jump on a bicycle is 5.85 meters, set by Tom Stoppard in 2008.

101-The La Cipale Vélodrome in Paris hosted the track cycling events of the 1900 Olympic Games.

102-The "Tour de l'Avenir" is a cycling race which showcases young talents and often serves as a springboard towards a professional career.

103-Belgium has produced many cycling champions, including Eddy Merckx, Johan Museeuw, and Tom Boonen.

104-The longest cycle path in the world is the "Route verte" in Quebec, Canada, with over 5,000 kilometers of cycle paths.

105-French rider Raymond Poulidor, nicknamed "Poupou", is famous for having finished on the second step of the Tour de France podium three times without ever winning it.

106-The first tandem bicycle was created in 1898, allowing two cyclists to pedal together.

107-The longest bicycle chain ever created was over 2,500 meters long.

108-The "Tour of California" is a cycling stage race in the United States that began in 2006.

109-The Tour de France is the third most watched sporting event in the world, after the FIFA World Cup and the Olympic Games.

110-Cyclocross riders often have to carry their bikes over impassable sections or ride them over obstacles.

111-The first derailleurs were operated by levers located on the horizontal bar of the bicycle frame.

112-The world record for the greatest distance traveled in 24 hours on a mountain bike is 814 kilometers, set by Brett Wolfe in 2019.

113-American cyclist Marshall "Major" Taylor became the first world cycling champion in 1899.

114-Sweden hosted the Road Cycling World Championships in 2020.

115-The bicycle is the most efficient means of transport in terms of energy spent per kilometer traveled.

116-Three-wheeled bicycles are sometimes called "tricycles" or "trikes".

117-The first pedal bicycle was invented by Pierre and Ernest Michaux in 1861.

118-The "Tour of Poland" is a stage cycling race which began in 1928.

119-The Tour de France was interrupted during World War I (1915-1918) and World War II (1940-1946).

120-Spanish rider Miguel Indurain won the Tour de France five consecutive times between 1991 and 1995.

121-The team time trial is an event where the riders of a team cycle together to achieve the best time. It is often contested during the Tour de France.

122-The "Tour de Yorkshire" is a cycle stage race in the United Kingdom which began in 2015.

123-Mountain biking was born in California in the 1970s.

124-The highest cycling trails in the world are found in the Peruvian mountains, reaching altitudes of over 5,000 meters.

125-The record for climbing Everest by bike is 7 hours and 11 minutes, set by Scott Beaumont in 2017.

126-The world record for the longest distance traveled in 24 hours on a recumbent bike is 1,219.84 kilometers, set by Ken Bonner in 2004.

127-Professional riders' bicycles are subject to strict rules regarding weight, they must weigh at least 6.8 kilograms.

128-American rider Lance Armstrong won seven consecutive Tours de France before his titles were stripped from him due to doping scandals.

129-The world record for the most kilometers traveled in 48 hours is 1,219.087 kilometers, set by Amanda Coker in 2016.

130-The bicycle is one of the most efficient means of transport in terms of the number of calories burned per kilometer traveled.

131-The term "fixie" refers to a fixed gear bicycle, where the pedals rotate at the same time as the rear wheel.

132-The "Tour Down Under" is the first race on the UCI World Tour calendar and takes place in Australia.

133-American cyclist Taylor Phinney is the son of two former professional cyclists, Davis Phinney and Connie Carpenter.

134-Italian rider Fausto Coppi was the first to win both the Tour de France and the Giro d'Italia in the same year, in 1949 and 1952.

135-The first yellow jersey of the Tour de France was worn by the Frenchman Eugène Christophe in 1919.

136-The "Tour of Qatar" was a stage cycling race known for its harsh wind conditions and extreme heat.

137-The "Giro d'Italia" is another of the Grand Tours of cycling, created in 1909.

138-Belgian rider Tom Boonen is nicknamed the "Tornado Tom" due to his exceptional skills in the spring classics.

139-The world record for the longest bunny hop on a bicycle is 1.4 meters, established by Benito Ros Charral in 2013.

140-The "Tour of the Basque Country" is a stage cycling race that features steep climbs and descents in the Spanish Basque Country.

141-The Tour de France has a cash prize for each stage, as well as for the overall winner.

142-The "Tour de Burgos" is a stage race in Spain which began in 1946.

143-The recumbent bicycle is a type of bicycle where the rider lies rather than seated, which reduces air resistance.

144-The world record for the most jumps on the bike in one minute is 67 jumps, set by David Schnabel in 2014.

145-The first green jersey of the Tour de France was worn by the Frenchman Désiré Keteleer in 1953.

146-The "Tour de Langkawi" is a stage cycling race which has taken place in Malaysia since 1996.

147-The most consecutive Tour de France victories is five, held by Jacques Anquetil, Eddy Merckx, Bernard Hinault, and Miguel Indurain.

148-British rider Chris Froome is one of the few to have won the Tour de France four times, achieving the feat in 2013, 2015, 2016 and 2017.

149-The largest stage victory at the Tour de France in terms of time difference was 35 minutes and 34 seconds, achieved by Albert Bourlon in 1947.

150-The "Clásica de San Sebastián" is a one-day classic in Spain that includes steep climbs and technical descents.